THE OCEAN LOVER'S QUOTATION BOOK

THE
OCEAN
LOVER'S
QUOTATION
BOOK

AN INSPIRED COLLECTION

CELEBRATING THE BEAUTY

& WONDERS OF THE SEA

Arranged by Jackie Corley

Improve your life. Change your world.
Connect with us at www.hatherleighpress.com

THE OCEAN LOVER'S QUOTATION BOOK

Text Copyright © 2023 Hatherleigh Press

Library of Congress Cataloging-in-Publication Data is available.
ISBN: 978-1-57826-939-6

Design by Carolyn Kasper

Printed in the United States
10 9 8 7 6 5 4 3 2 1

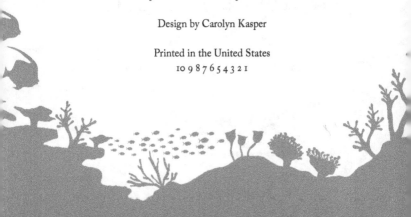

The sea, once it casts its spell, holds one
in its net of wonder forever.

—JACQUES YVES COUSTEAU

CONTENTS

INTRODUCTION

THERE'S SOMETHING COMFORTING ABOUT staring at the broad, blue ocean. Hearing the rhythmic crashing of the waves, arriving on the shoreline and pulling back again.

The ocean is a place where time stands still. The infinite horizon, the waves that have lapped the beach for millions of years...they stir something primitive inside of us. At once, we're looking at the same image our ancestors saw and which future generations will someday experience. This sense of connection roots us firmly in the present and puts us at ease.

Hence why a simple beach vacation becomes an opportunity for a much-needed battery recharge. The stresses of everyday life fade into the background. We find rejuvenation and peace standing along the shoreline.

Or perhaps the tranquil surface of the ocean is so mesmerizing to us because of the mysteries that lurk beneath. Destructive storms can unleash the full wrath of a wild sea, yet in its depths lies a world of aquatic life that humans rarely get to see.

Hidden from sight deep below, the beauty, magic and force of the ocean has captivated sailors, writers and philosophers for thousands of years. The quotes in this collection reflect our long-held love affair with the ocean.

THE
OCEAN
LOVER'S
QUOTATION
BOOK

An Extension of the Soul

We feel a kinship with the ocean. Perhaps it harkens back to our sense of being submerged in the womb, but the ocean feels like an extension of our basic nature. We are more contemplative and centered when we're near the shoreline.

Every time I slip into the ocean, it's like going home.

— SYLVIA EARLEE

We are tied to the ocean. And when we go back to the sea, whether it is to sail or to watch—we are going back from whence we came.

— JOHN F. KENNEDY

You're not a wave, you're a part of the ocean.

— MITCH ALBOM

The voice of the sea speaks to the soul. The touch of the sea is sensuous, enfolding the body in its soft, close embrace.

— KATE CHOPIN

The sea lives in every one of us.

— ROBERT WYLAND

In still moments by the sea life seems large-drawn and simple. It is there we can see into ourselves.

— ROLF EDBERG

For whatever we lose (like a you or a me),
It's always our self we find in the sea.

— E.E. CUMMINGS

Those who live by the sea can hardly form a
single thought of which the sea would not
be part.

— HERMANN BROCH

Out of water, I am nothing.

— DUKE KAHANAMOKU

The cure for anything is salt water—sweat, tears, or the sea.

— ISAK DINESEN

Life is a wave, which in no two consecutive moments of its existence is composed of the same particles.

— JOHN TYNDALL

The ocean has a life of its own. Its tides, whirlpools, currents and eddies are a testament to its conflicting emotions.

— ANTHONY T. HINCKS

The sea is emotion incarnate. It loves, hates, and weeps. It defies all attempts to capture it with words and rejects all shackles. No matter what you say about it, there is always that which you can't.

— CHRISTOPHER PAOLINI

As the oceans go, so do we.

— DAVID DOUBILET

You stand next to the sea and you're in touch with all your longings and all your losses.

— ELIZABETH HAY

To me, the sea is like a person—like a child that I've known a long time. It sounds crazy, I know, but when I swim in the sea I talk to it. I never feel alone when I'm out there.

— GERTRUDE EDERLE

Every time we walk along a beach some ancient urge disturbs us so that we find ourselves shedding shoes and garments or scavenging among seaweed and whitened timbers like the homesick refugees of a long war.

— LOREN EISELEY

We are all connected to the ocean. Without healthy oceans, no life, not even on land, can exist.

— JEAN-MICHEL COUSTEAU

The three great elemental sounds in nature are the sound of rain, the sound of wind in a primeval wood, and the sound of outer ocean on a beach.

— HENRY BESTON

The waves of the sea help me get back to me.

— JILL DAVIS

You must not lose faith in humanity. Humanity is an ocean; if a few drops of the ocean are dirty, the ocean does not become dirty.

— MAHATMA GANDHI

With every drop of water you drink, every breath you take, you're connected to the sea. No matter where on Earth you live.

— SYLVIA EARLE

We are a blue planet and an ocean world.

— NAINOA THOMPSON

Just as the wave cannot exist for itself, but is ever a part of the heaving surface of the ocean, so must I never live my life for itself, but always in the experience which is going on around me.

— ALBERT SCHWEITZER

If the ocean can calm itself, so can you. We are both saltwater mixed with air.

— NAYYIRAH WAHEED

I need the sea because it teaches me.

— PABLO NERUDA

You can either see yourself as a wave in the ocean or you can see yourself as the ocean.

— OPRAH WINFREY

The ocean stirs the heart, inspires the imagination and brings eternal joy to the soul.

— ROBERT WYLAND

I pray to be like the ocean, with soft currents, maybe waves at times. More and more, I want the consistency rather than the highs and the lows.

— DREW BARRYMORE

Life is like the ocean, it goes up and down.

— VANESSA PARADIS

Your thoughts, feelings and sensations are the waves of the ocean—coming and going. There are big strong waves and there are soft gentle waves; they are all water and all part of the ocean.

— ROSE-MARIE SOROKIN

You never enjoy the world aright, till the Sea itself floweth in your veins.

— THOMAS TRAHERNE

Health to the ocean means health for us.

— SYLVIA EARLE

The heart of man is very much like the sea, it has its storms, it has its tides and in its depths it has its pearls too.

— VINCENT VAN GOGH

You can't stop the waves, but you can learn to surf.

— JON KABAT-ZINN

Why do we love the sea? It is because it has some potent power to make us think things we like to think.

— ROBERT HENRI

For her the ocean was more than a dream, it was a place she needed to visit to find herself. And when she returned to the city, you could see the sun in her eyes, the wind in her hair, and taste in the infinite salt on her lips.

—JOSE CHAVES

He always thought of the sea as 'la mar' which is what people call her in Spanish when they love her.

—ERNEST HEMINGWAY

There's magic in the water that draws all men away from the land, that leads them over hills, down creeks and streams and rivers to the sea.

—HERMAN MELVILLE

Awe-Inspiring
Power

*From the Greek myths of Poseidon to the
seafaring thrillers seen in epic Hollywood
films, the overwhelming power of the ocean
has long captured the imagination. We feel a
sense of wonder and humility when standing
beside the sea.*

The sea does not like to be restrained.

— RICK RIORDAN

The solemn, wonderful, majestic ocean! It exalts, but only to crush me under a sense of its grandeur—boundless, everlasting, pitiless of my insignificance. Wherein does it differ from me? In immensity of breadth and depth. What does it give me? A sense of infinity, and of the abyss which divides me from it.

— MADAME SWETCHINE

Roll on, deep and dark blue ocean, roll. Ten thousand fleets sweep over thee in vain. Man marks the earth with ruin, but his control stops with the shore.

— LORD BYRON

The ocean makes me feel really small and it makes me put my whole life into perspective...it humbles you and makes you feel almost like you've been baptized. I feel born again when I get out of the ocean.

— BEYONCÉ KNOWLES

The sea speaks a language polite people never repeat. It is a colossal scavenger slang and has no respect.

— CARL SANDBURG

There's a magical energy and power from the ocean.

—JO BEVERLEY

The sea is the same as it has been since before men ever went on it in boats.

— ERNEST HEMINGWAY

There was a magic about the sea. People were drawn to it. People wanted to love by it, swim in it, play in it, look at it. It was a living thing that was as unpredictable as a great stage actor: it could be calm and welcoming, opening its arms to embrace its audience one moment, but then could explode with its stormy tempers, flinging people around, wanting them out, attacking coastlines, breaking down islands.

— CECELIA AHERN

The sea drives truth into a man like salt.

— HILAIRE BELLOC

The sea has boundless patience.

— CRAIG ROBERTSON

Without water, our planet would be one of the billions of lifeless rocks floating endlessly in the vastness of the inky-black void.

— FABIEN COUSTEAU

When people who love the ocean come together, they can achieve extraordinary things.

— FRANCES BEINECKE

If you live a life of make-believe, your life isn't worth anything until you do something that does challenge your reality. And to me, sailing the open ocean is a real challenge, because it's life or death.

— MORGAN FREEMAN

Most of us, I suppose, are a little nervous of the sea. No matter what its smiles may be, we doubt its friendship.

— H.M. TOMLINSON

The ocean is a wilderness reaching round the globe, wilder than a Bengal jungle, and fuller of monsters, washing the very wharves of our cities and the gardens of our sea-side residences.

— HENRY DAVID THOREAU

Go strip off your clothes that are a nuisance in this mellow clime. Get in and wrestle with the sea; wing your heels with the skill and power that reside in you, hit the sea's breakers, master them, and ride upon their backs as a king should.

— JACK LONDON

There is an energy to the ocean in particular, an element of danger that requires a giving over of self, that makes swimming in heavy water a kind of holy communion. I see swimming as a way to get to know a place with an intimacy that I otherwise wouldn't have. To swim in the ocean is to immerse myself in wildness, to feel the way the water rises and falls like breath.

— BONNIE TSUI

No water, no life. No blue, no green.

— SYLVIA EARLE

The ocean is the throbbing heart of the universe, and its every wave a mound over those who have no graves.

— MISS C. TALBOTT

The sea knows no limits, makes no concessions. It has given us everything and it can take everything away from us.

— JOHN AJVIDE LINDQVIST

Water is the softest of all things, yet it is the most powerful. The ocean patiently allows all things to flow into it. It is always flexible.

— WAYNE DYER

You never really know what's coming. A small wave, or maybe a big one. All you can really do is hope that when it comes, you can surf over it, instead of drowning in its monstrosity.

— ALYSHA SPEER

Water is the driving force in nature.

— LEONARDO DA VINCI

Water always goes where it wants to go, and nothing, in the end, can stand against it. Water is patient. Dripping water wears away a stone.

— MARGARET ATWOOD

Wild waves rise and fall when they arrive and that's what makes the calm sea alive.

— MUNIA KHAN

You can never cross the ocean until you have the courage to lose sight of the shore.

—CHRISTOPHER COLUMBUS

The ocean is an object of no small terror.

— EDMUND BURKE

Never trust the calm sea when she shows her false alluring smile.

— LUCRETIUS

What would an ocean be without a monster lurking in the dark? It would be like sleep without dreams.

— WERNER HERZOG

The ocean is a mighty harmonist.

— WILLIAM WORDSWORTH

Those who did not know the ocean well forgot its solidity, its brutality. When it slammed into them with the force of cold metal they were appalled.

— ROBERT GALBRAITH

If we look at the ocean in a calm, there is something imposing in its aspect; stretched out in its sleeping tranquility, but looking fearfully deep, and its silence seems like that of the lion when crouching for its prey.

— JENNY M. PARKER

Waves are the voices of tides. Tides are life. They bring new food for shore creatures and take ships out to sea. They are the ocean's pulse, and our own heartbeat.

— TAMORA PIERCE

I wish I could describe the feeling of being at sea, the anguish, frustration, and fear, the beauty that accompanies threatening spectacles, the spiritual communion with creatures in whose domain I sail.

— STEVE CALLAHAN

Nor is there in the whole range of nature a grander or more magnificent scene than the ocean in a storm, when deep calls unto deep, and its liquid mountains roll and break against each other, when it dashes to pieces, in the wantonness of its power, the strongest, structures which man can rear for the purpose of floating over its billows; then it is that the proudest and bravest tremble and quail at the roaring and thunder of its waters.

— PETER WHITTLE

The ocean humbles you. You can go and win a world title, but you're never going to beat the ocean.

— STEPHANIE GILMORE

The sea, washing the equator and the poles, offers its perilous aid, and the power and empire that follow it ... "Beware of me," it says, "but if you can hold me, I am the key to all the lands."

— RALPH WALDO EMERSON

MYSTERY & MAGIC

The depths of the ocean remain one of the last underexplored frontiers on the planet. No wonder life beneath its surface seems magical, mysterious and otherworldly.

The sea is a place of mystery. One by one, the mysteries of yesterday have been solved. But the solution seems always to bring with it another, perhaps a deeper mystery. I doubt that the last, final mysteries of the sea will ever be resolved. In fact, I cherish a very unscientific hope that they will not be.

— RACHEL CARSON

I have always been fascinated by the ocean, to dip a limb beneath its surface and know that I'm touching eternity, that it goes on forever until it begins here again.

— LAUREN DESTEFANO

The sea is as near as we come to another world.

— ANNE STEVENSON

The sea pronounces something, over and over,
in a hoarse whisper; I cannot quite make it out.

— ANNIE DILLARD

Waves are toys from God.

— CLAY MARZO

There's nothing wrong with enjoying looking at the surface of the ocean itself, except that when you finally see what goes on underwater, you realize that you've been missing the whole point of the ocean. Staying on the surface all the time is like going to the circus and staring at the outside of the tent.

— DAVE BARRY

The ocean is this beautiful, unexplored place. Why on Earth everyone isn't down there, I don't know.

— GRAHAM HAWKES

If the private life of the sea could ever be transposed onto paper, it would talk not about rivers or rain or glaciers or of molecules of oxygen and hydrogen, but of the millions of encounters its waters have shared with creatures of another nature.

— FEDERICO CHINI

As with anything worthy of investment, we must also continue our efforts to understand the ocean better. To date, less than ten percent of it has been thoroughly mapped, and only one percent has been actively explored.

— GARY E. KNELL

Ocean is more ancient than the mountains, and freighted with the memories and the dreams of Time.

— H. P. LOVECRAFT

You could start now, and spend another forty years learning about the sea without running out of new things to know.

— PETER BENCHLEY

Be alone with the sea for it is there you will find answers to questions you didn't realize exist.

— KHANG KIJARRO NGUYEN

The sea possesses a power over one's moods that has the effect of a will. The sea can hypnotize. Nature in general can do so.

— HENRIK IBSEN

Would you learn the secret of the sea? Only those who brave its dangers, comprehend its mystery!

— HENRY WADSWORTH
LONGFELLOW

The edge of the sea is a strange and beautiful place.

— RACHEL CARSON

My soul is full of longing for the secret of the sea, and the heart of the great ocean sends a thrilling pulse through me.

— HENRY WADSWORTH
LONGFELLOW

There is, one knows not what sweet mystery about this sea, whose gently awful stirrings seem to speak of some hidden soul beneath.

— HERMAN MELVILLE

Mystery of mysteries, water and air are right there before us in the sea. Every time I view the sea, I feel a calming sense of security, as if visiting my ancestral home; I embark on a voyage of seeing.

— HIROSHI SUGIMOTO

The sea, once it casts its spell, holds one in its net of wonder forever.

— JACQUES YVES COUSTEAU

Every time you dive, you hope you'll see something new—some new species. Sometimes the ocean gives you a gift, sometimes it doesn't.

— JAMES CAMERON

Don't try to describe the ocean if you've never seen it.

— JIMMY BUFFETT

Rich and various gems inlay
The unadorned bosom of the deep.

— JOHN MILTON

I love the sea's sounds and the way it reflects the sky. The colors that shimmer across its surface are unbelievable. This, combined with the color of the water over white sand, surprises me every time.

—JOHN DYER

What are the wild waves saying,
Sister, the whole day long,
That ever amid our playing
I hear but their low, lone song?

—JOSEPH E. CARPENTER

To their inhabitants, the sea is everything. Their hopes and fears, their gains and losses, their joys and sorrows, are linked with it; and the largeness of the ocean has molded their feelings and their characters. They are in a measure partakers of its immensity and its mystery. The commonest of their men have wrestled with the powers of the air, and the might of wind, and wave, and icy cold. The weakest of their women have felt the hallowing touch of sudden calamity, and of long, lonely, life-and-death watches.

— AMELIA E. BARR

The great depths of the ocean are entirely unknown to us; soundings cannot reach them. What fanes in those remote depths, what beings live twelve or fifteen miles beneath the surface of the waters, what is the organization of the animals we can scarcely conjecture?

—JULES VERNE

If there is magic on this planet, it is contained in water.

—LOREN EISELEY

The beauty and mystery of the ocean fills our lives with wonders vast beyond our imagination.

— M. L. BORGES

Let the waves carry you where the light cannot.

— MOHIT KAUSHIK

More wonderful than the lore of old men and the lore of books is the secret lore of the ocean. Blue, green, grey, white, or black; smooth, ruffled, or mountainous; that ocean is not silent.

— H. P. LOVECRAFT

After a visit to the beach, it's hard to believe that we live in a material world.

— PAM SHAW

The ocean and the wind and the stars and the moon will all teach you many things.

— JANE ROBERTS

The sea is an underwater museum still awaiting its visitors.

— PHILLIP DIOLE

Full many a gem of purest ray serene,
The dark unfathomed caves of ocean bear.

— THOMAS GRAY

Coastal people never really know what the ocean symbolizes to landlocked inland people—what a great distant dream it is, present but unseen in the deepest level of subconsciousness, and when they arrive at the ocean and the conscious images are compared with the subconscious dream there is a sense of defeat at having come so far to be stopped by a mystery that can never be fathomed. The source of it all.

— ROBERT M. PIRSIG

In one drop of water are found all the secrets of all the oceans; in one aspect of you are found all the aspects of existence.

— KAHLIL GIBRAN JR.

I want everybody to go jump in the ocean to see for themselves how beautiful it is, how important it is to get acquainted with fish swimming in the ocean, rather than just swimming with lemon slices and butter.

— SYLVIA EARLE

The sea does not reward those who are too anxious, too greedy, or too impatient.... Patience, patience, patience, is what the sea teaches. Patience and faith. One should lie empty, open, choiceless as a beach—waiting for a gift from the sea.

— ANNE MORROW LINDBERGH

To me, the sea is a continual miracle; The fishes that swim–the rocks–the motion of the waves–the ships, with men in them, What stranger miracles are there?

— WALT WHITMAN

There, amidst its inmost recesses, amidst its
caverns and hidden depths, are contained
secrets which can never be divulged; there the
mighty monsters of the deep, many of them
unknown to us, play and sport; there the beautiful beds of pearl and coral hide their brightest
treasures; there the tough and hardy seaweed
clings to its isolated and solitary rock, fathoms
and fathoms below the surface of the water:
there, doubtless, lies many a beautiful spot,
which, if it could be elevated from beneath
the superincumbent weight of waters, would
be found some beautiful island, glittering with
all the treasures of the ocean.

— PETER WHITTLE

TRANQUILITY & PEACE

The sound of the waves is a natural, soothing symphony. When we look to relax and recharge, the beach is often the first place that comes to mind. There's something restorative about standing beside the ocean.

From birth, man carries the weight of gravity on his shoulders. He is bolted to earth. But man has only to sink beneath the surface and he is free.

— JACQUES YVES COUSTEAU

The calming movement of the sea along with the restless ocean breeze gently caresses me creating a soothing trance which lulls me to a place of peace.

— M. L. BORGES

I wanted freedom, open air and adventure.
I found it on the sea.

— ALAIN GERBAULT

One cannot collect all the beautiful shells on
the beach. One can collect only a few, and they
are more beautiful if they are few.

— ANNE MORROW LINDBERGH

Being out there in the ocean, God's creation,
it's like a gift He has given us to enjoy.

— BETHANY HAMILTON

There's nothing more beautiful than the way the ocean refuses to stop kissing the shoreline, no matter how many times it's sent away.

— SARAH KAY

Find comfort in the rhythm of the sea.

— CHARLOTTE ERIKSSON

The sea will grant each man new hope, and sleep will bring dreams of home.

— CHRISTOPHER COLUMBUS

If everyone could just live near the ocean,
I think we'd all be happier. It's hard to be
down about anything knee-deep in the sand.

— CRYSTAL WOODS

On the beach, you can live in bliss.

— DENNIS WILSON

I like it when you're under the ocean, and all
you can feel is calm.

— FARRAH FAWCETT

I miss the beach, the peace it brings you. I love the sound and smell of the sea.

— GENESIS RODRIGUEZ

I need the sun, sand and ocean to rejuvenate my spirit, the food to enliven my body and all of the familiar places, friends and family to revitalize my soul. I go for replenishment. For a kind of love that I truly know. For a place of belonging, always.

— GRACE GEALEY

A kiss on the beach when there is a full moon
is the closest thing to heaven.

— H. JACKSON BROWN, JR.

I could never stay long enough on the shore;
the tang of the untainted, fresh, and free sea
air was like a cool, quieting thought.

— HELEN KELLER

To go out with the setting sun on an empty
beach is to truly embrace your solitude.

— JEANNE MOREAU

The ocean has always been a salve to my soul.

— JIMMY BUFFETT

That the sea is one of the most beautiful and magnificent sights in Nature, all admit.

— JOHN JOLY

Have you ever just sat and listened to the waves rolling in? It is like an orchestra, beautiful relaxing music.

— CATHERINE PULSIFER

Total physical and mental inertia are highly agreeable, much more so than we allow ourselves to imagine. A beach not only permits such inertia but enforces it, thus neatly eliminating all problems of guilt. It is now the only place in our overly active world that does.

—JOHN KENNETH GALBRAITH

Dance with the waves, move with the sea, let the rhythm of the water set your soul free.

—CHRISTY ANN MARTINE

On the surface of the ocean, men wage war and destroy each other; but down here, just a few feet beneath the surface, there is a calm and peace, unmolested by man.

— JULES VERNE

I miss the ocean. I miss diving into the cold water and coming out a new man....Showers are okay, but there's nothing quite like being in the ocean.

— ANGUS STONE

Sometimes in the morning, when it's a good surf, I go out there, and I don't feel like it's a bad world.

— KARY MULLIS

The ocean is a very, very beautiful place. It is God's gift to us.

— LYNNE COX

The beach is a place of solitude where I can set my spirit free and relax.

— M. L. BORGES

A beach walk is for stretching your legs and your mind, for looking at life with newfound eyes.

— SANDY GINGRAS

I go to the ocean to calm down, to reconnect with the creator, to just be happy.

— NNEDI OKORAFOR

The ocean is so magnificent, peaceful, and awesome. The rest of the world disappears for me when I'm on a wave.

— PAUL WALKER

Every time I stand before a beautiful beach, its waves seem to whisper to me: If you choose the simple things and find joy in nature's simple treasures, life and living need not be so hard.

— PSYCHE ROXAS-MENDOZA

When anxious, uneasy and bad thoughts come, I go to the sea, and the sea drowns them out with its great wide sounds, cleanses me with its noise, and imposes a rhythm upon everything in me that is bewildered and confused.

— RAINER MARIA RILKE

At night, when the sky is full of stars and the sea is still you get the wonderful sensation that you are floating in space.

— NATALIE WOOD

At the beach, life is different. Time doesn't move hour to hour but mood to moment. We live by the currents, plan by the tides and follow the sun.

— SANDY GINGRAS

I love the ocean. I've always liked the blue, so tranquil and peaceful and gliding. And the fear of it.

— SIOUXSIE SIOUX

Ever since I was a child I've felt connected to water: lakes, rivers, streams—I love to jump in and swim around. But it's the ocean where I go for rejuvenation, revelation, and solace.

— SUSAN COHN ROCKEFELLER

Success underwater depends mostly on how you conduct yourself. Diving can be the most relaxing experience in the world. Your weight seems to disappear. Space travel will be available only to a few individuals for some time, but the oceans are available to almost everyone—now.

— SYLVIA EARLE

At the beach—time you enjoyed wasting, is not wasted.

— T. S. ELIOT

There is something about the ocean that never fails to amaze me, the way she never fails to kiss the shores even though she is sent away, the way her waves can be both calm and terrifying and the way she never fails to soothe my soul.

— TILICIA HARIDAT

Looking out over the ocean you can see reflections of God.

— CATHERINE PULSIFER

Once your feet have touched the warm sun drenched sand of the seashore you will never ever be the same.

— PATSY GANT

Walking on the beach brings a smile to my face. The beach where children play and parents are not in the rat-race. Everyone is happy on that day!

— CATHERINE PULSIFER

Dwelling beside a body of water is tonic for the weary psyche. Sea smells, sea birds, sea wrack, sands—alternately cool, warm, moist and dry—a taste of brine and the presence of the rocking, slopping bluegraygreen spit-flecked waters, has the effect of rinsing the emotions, bathing the outlook, bleaching the conscience.

— ROGER ZELAZNY

The biggest sin in the world would be if I lost my love for the ocean.

— LAIRD HAMILTON

Each kiss of an ocean wave is passed along, as long as there is life on and in the seas.

— ANTHONY T. HINCKS

One learns first of all in beach living the art of shedding; how little one can get along with, not how much.

— ANNE MORROW LINDBERGH

Smell the sea and feel the sky. Let your soul
and spirit fly.

—VAN MORRISON

The high meridian of the day is past,
And Ocean now, reflecting the calm Heaven,
Is of cerulean hue; and murmurs low
The tide of ebb, upon the level sands.

—CHARLOTTE SMITH

Wondrous Expanse of the Sea

The seemingly endless ocean horizon reminds us how massive it is and how small we are beside it. The expansiveness of the ocean leaves us with a sense of wonder.

Limitless and immortal, the waters are the beginning and end of all things on earth.

— HEINRICH ZIMMER

To stand at the edge of the sea, to sense the ebb and flow of the tides, to feel the breath of a mist moving over a great salt marsh, to watch the flight of shore birds that have swept up and down the surf lines of the continents for untold thousands of years, to see the running of the old eels and the young shad to the sea, is to have knowledge of things that are as nearly eternal as any earthly life can be.

— RACHEL CARSON

Why is it that scuba divers and surfers are some of the strongest advocates of ocean conservation? Because they've spent time in and around the ocean, and they've personally seen the beauty, the fragility, and even the degradation of our planet's blue heart.

—SYLVIA EARLE

There is wisdom in waves.

—GERRY LOPEZ

There is no new wave, only the sea.

—CLAUDE CHABROL

The sea-shore is a sort of neutral ground, a most advantageous point from which to contemplate this world. It is even a trivial place. The waves forever rolling to the land are too far-travelled and untamable to be familiar. Creeping along the endless beach amid the sun-squall and the foam, it occurs to us that we, too, are the product of sea-slime.

— HENRY DAVID THOREAU

The ocean is a central image. It is the symbolism of a great journey.

— ENYA

Water seeks its own level. Look at them—the Tigris, the Euphrates, the Mississippi, the Amazon, the Yangtze. The World's great rivers, and every one of them finds its way to the ocean.

— ALISON MCGHEE

The sea! the sea! the open sea! The blue, the fresh, the ever free! Without a mark, without a bound, It runneth the earth's wide regions round; It plays with the clouds; it mocks the skies; Or like a cradled creature lies.

— BRYAN WALLER PROCTER

Hail, thou multitudinous ocean! Thy fluctuating waters wash the varied shores of the world, and while they disjoin nations whom a nearer connection would involve in eternal war, they circulate their arts and their labors, and give health and plenty to mankind.

— CHRISTOPH STURM

If you want to build a ship, don't drum up people to collect wood and don't assign them tasks and work, but rather teach them to long for the endless immensity of the sea.

— ANTOINE DE
SAINT-EXUPERY

What is any ocean but a multitude of drops?

— DAVID MITCHELL

I have an immoderate passion for water; for the sea, though so vast, so restless, so beyond one's comprehension.

— GUY DE MAUPASSANT

You will love the ocean. It makes you feel so...I don't know. Small, but not in a bad way. Small because you realize you're part of something bigger.

— LAUREN MYRACLE

We ourselves feel that what we are doing is just a drop in the ocean. But the ocean would be less because of that missing drop.

— MOTHER TERESA

I think people had somehow gotten the sense that we have explored everything, when that isn't the case. We so know so little about the ocean, and so much of it is being destroyed.

— JAMES CAMERON

The ocean is not just blank blue space but rather the habitat for amazing wildlife, and we have to take care how we use it. If we want to keep having the goods and services it provides, we have to treat it more carefully in terms of fishing and dumping.

— CARL SAFINA

All rivers pay homage to the ocean for it lies lowest.

— JEFFREY FRY

How inappropriate to call this planet Earth when it is quite clearly Ocean.

— ARTHUR C. CLARKE

Miles of ocean, and oh, the vastness of it, shadows and salt, fierce dark water filled with alien emptiness and the monsters that lived there.

— CASSANDRA CLARE

As a species, we've always been discoverers and adventurers, and space and the deep ocean are some of the last frontiers.

— PAUL ALLEN

The beach is truly home, its broad expanse of sand as welcoming as a mother's open arms. What's more, this landscape, which extends as far as the eye can see, always reminds me of possibility.

— JOAN ANDERSON

The sea is everything. It covers seven tenths of the terrestrial globe. Its breath is pure and healthy. It is an immense desert, where man is never lonely, for he feels life stirring on all sides.

— JULES VERNE

The sea is a desert of waves, a wilderness of water.

— LANGSTON HUGHES

That's what I think people sense when they get hooked by surfing—hooked by their relationship with the ocean. All of a sudden, they're part of something that's bigger than them.

— NICK CARROLL

When I forget how talented God is, I look to the sea.

— WHOOPI GOLDBERG

Ah, well, then you've never stood on a beach as the waves came crashing in, the water stretching out from you until it's beyond sight, moving and blue and alive and so much bigger than even the black beyond seems because the ocean hides what it contains.

— PATRICK NESS

In every outthrust headland, in every curving beach, in every grain of sand there is the story of the earth.

— RACHEL CARSON

No nation ever had two better friends that we have. You know who they are? The Atlantic and Pacific oceans.

— WILL ROGERS

Whenever I look at the ocean, I always want to talk to people, but when I'm talking to people, I always want to look at the ocean.

— HARUKI MURAKAMI

There's never an end for the sea.

— SAMUEL BECKETT

The most interesting feeling when watching an ocean is this: It seems like something will come from the distant horizon but actually nothing comes!

— MEHMET MURAT ILDAN

The sea, the great unifier, is man's only hope. Now, as never before, the old phrase has a literal meaning: we are all in the same boat.

— JACQUES YVES COUSTEAU

Individually, we are one drop. Together, we are an ocean.

— RYUNOSUKE SATORO

I have always been fascinated by the ocean, to dip a limb beneath its surface and know that I'm touching eternity, that it goes on forever until it begins here again.

— LAUREN DESTEFANO

Behold the Sea,
The opaline, the plentiful and strong,
Yet beautiful as is the rose in June,
Fresh as the trickling rainbow of July;
Sea full of food, the nourisher of kinds,
Purger of earth, and medicine of men;
Creating a sweet climate by my breath,
Washing out harms and griefs from memory,
And, in my mathematic ebb and flow,
Giving a hint of that which changes not.

— RALPH WALDO EMERSON

CONCLUSION

T HE OCEAN HAS EVER stimulated the imagination. From ancient mariners to vacation beachgoers, people have been drawn to the sight and smell and sound of open water.

More than a source of livelihood or leisure, however, the enduring impact of the ocean is the way it connects us to something larger than ourselves. The ocean provides us with a sense of peace while at the same time awing and humbling us with its tremendous power. Its crashing waves can lull us to sleep just as easily as they can swirl into a furious storm that destroys all in its path. This duality is part of what's so entrancing about the ocean.

Whether you're a frequent ocean visitor or long to experience it, the quotes in this collection are meant to serve as a touchstone for the mysterious, hypnotic pull of the sea. Refer back to it whenever you long to dip your toes into the water and feel the spray of salt water against your cheek!